*A Cat's Little
Instruction
Book*

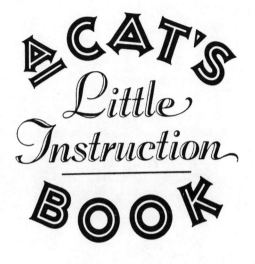

A CAT'S Little Instruction BOOK

LEIGH W. RUTLEDGE

GALAHAD BOOKS
NEW YORK

First Galahad Books edition published in 2000.

Galahad Books
A division of BBS Publishing Corporation
386 Park Avenue South
New York, NY 10016

Galahad Books is a registered trademark
of BBS Publishing Corporation.

Published by arrangement with the author.

Library of Congress Catalog Card Number: 99-75367

ISBN: 1-57866-083-1

Printed in the United States of America.

To Beardsley, Spitfire,
and Dr. Tom Bird

1. Always lick after meals.

2. When in doubt, chase something.

3. Keep your tail away from stoves, candles, lit cigarettes, garbage disposals, automatic dishwasher doors, children, rocking chairs, and dogs. Remember, God only gave you one tail—take good care of it.

4. Be adorable.

5. Worry about courage, cleanliness, and hair balls.

6. *Don't* worry about what other cats think of you. Remember, the cats who often do the most with their lives are the ones who were laughed at, ridiculed, or made fun of as kittens.

7. Stay out of automobile engines.

8. Stay out of open windows during thunderstorms.

9. Stay indoors on Halloween and the Fourth of July.

10. Surprise someone by hiding in the clothes hamper.

11. Avoid the temptation to spend all day waiting expectantly by the birdbath.

12. Christmas trees were meant to be climbed.

13. Long naps never go out of fashion.

14. Just say no to catnip.

15. The three Great Lies of Life are:

1. "The check is in the mail."

2. "All I want is one kiss."

3. "It'll be all right, just get in the carrying case."

16. Avoid cleaning your private parts in public places.

17. Never make love in the streets.

18. Forgive your enemies—but only after you've given them a couple of swats.

19. Never go to a veterinarian who doesn't have cats himself.

20. Never go back to a veterinarian who discusses his or her stock portfolio while taking your temperature.

21. Don't run to the vet's for every little ache and pain. Ninety percent of your medical problems will get better on their own, regardless of what you take or do for them.

22. Remember, no matter how much they love you, all human beings are biased to their own species.

23. Never go to bed with a resentful heart or a dirty face.

24. Get your booster shots every year on schedule.

25. Learn to recognize the sound of cereal being poured into a bowl; milk usually follows.

26. Be astonishingly mysterious.

27. Never be afraid to seek center stage.

28. Look *in* to people as well as *at* them.

29. When depressed or confused, try lying on your back with your legs in the air; sometimes the world just looks better upside down.

30. No matter what you've done wrong, always try to make it look like the dog did it.

31. Sniff every stranger.

32. Never take a nap in a parked car, or you may wake up and find yourself being carried off to a faraway place.

33. Avoid antifreeze, tinsel, broken Christmas tree ornaments, straight pins, paper clips, strange pills lying on the bathroom floor, styrofoam packing nuggets (they can clog you up), and mice you suspect have just eaten d-Con rat poison.

34. Help with jigsaw puzzles.

35. Sleep in a flowerbed to stay cool on hot summer days.

36. Cuddle with someone you love on snowy afternoons.

37. Avoid like the plague any person who has, within the last twelve months, picked you up and shaken you adoringly.

38. Forgive people who babble baby talk in your face. They're only repeating the mistakes someone else taught them.

39. Never brood about the past. If you're ever tempted to, take a good hard look at the humans around you. They do it all the time—are *they* happy?

40. Learn the difference
between idleness and
repose—one wastes time,
the other luxuriates in it.

41. When playing games with your own kittens, let them get the best of you.

42. When playing games with someone else's kittens, beat them up.

43. Never, ever let anyone floss your teeth—unless you're unconscious or dead.

44. When a friend wants to
lick you, let them.

45. Avoid vacuum cleaners.

46. Stay off swimming pool diving boards.

47. Let sleeping dogs lie.

48. Remember that foxes, skunks, and owls usually have the last word in any confrontation.

49. Be a friend to people who have suffered grief, rejection, abuse, financial loss, or recent illness. In moments of personal tragedy, human beings tend to run away from one another—learn from their bad example.

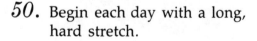

50. Begin each day with a long, hard stretch.

51. Never sleep too close to a fireplace that has a fire going in it.

52. Never chew on electrical cords or wires.

53. Never eat raw meat or stale leftovers. Always ask yourself: If it isn't something humans would feed their kids, why are they feeding it to *you*?

54. Leave every dog with the impression that you are a lion cub who will be back to get him when you grow up.

55. It's only an old wives' tale that a little kitty litter tossed out of the cat box wards off the Devil. Make an effort to keep the area around your cat box clean.

56. Don't sit or sleep on the microwave when it's in operation. You don't know *what* it might be doing to you.

57. Take time to savor the view from every window in your house.

58. Watch out for human feet. (They won't watch out for you.)

59. Always clean between your toes.

60. Choose your loyalties carefully, but once you've chosen them put your heart and soul into them.

61. Ignore any and all silly propaganda about cats being aloof, amoral, sinister, stupid, and false-hearted. The people who believe such things are themselves more often than not aloof, amoral, sinister, stupid, and false-hearted.

62. Run away and hide the moment you hear any group of human beings speculating about whether cats always land on their feet.

63. Stay out of the rain.

64. Stay out of the snow.

65. Stay out of the clothes dryer.

66. Become a force to be reckoned with—but don't run it into the ground.

67. Seek out good hiding
places.

68. Treat yourself to a nap in
the sock drawer once in
awhile.

69. When scaling trees, never be satisfied with the lowest limb—always aim straight for the top. However, keep in mind that most fire departments no longer get cats out of trees. If you get stuck, you're pretty much on your own.

70. Explore your territory, but don't become a fanatic about marking it.

71. Avoid packs of roving children. A child alone can sometimes be dealt with, but once in a herd they often turn into berserk little creatures trying to impress one another.

72. Look both ways before crossing the street. Never *dart*. Better yet, don't cross streets.

73. Don't bite your nails.

74. Roll in the dirt at least once a week to maintain a healthy and beautiful coat.

75. After the age of ten, cut back on the amount of fish and red meat you consume.

76. Learn the difference
between a pair of shoes
and a litter box.

77. Never worry about medical or cat food bills. Someone else will pay them.

78. Don't be fooled by cat furniture—tiny beds, cramped baskets, etc.—sold in pet stores. Human furniture is always more plush and comfortable.

79. Remember that every baby bird you encounter has a mother who would be heartbroken if you ate it.

80. Let your emotions get the best of you sometimes.

81. Climb the living room drapes to develop upper-body strength.

82. Resist an urge to leap onto the ceiling fan, especially when it's in motion.

83. Never be discouraged by the words "No," "Stop that," or "Bad cat."

84. Never be overly concerned when someone screams, "If you ever do that again, I'm going to make you an outdoor cat once and for all!" It's almost always an idle threat.

85. To make a lasting impression at parties, jump in the onion dip, or stick your head in the punch bowl and start slurping loudly. If all else fails, perch yourself like a vulture on the arm of a sofa and leave all the guests with the impression that if they don't finish the hors d'oeuvres soon, *you* will.

86. Own nothing, and be owned by no one.

87. Cultivate bedroom eyes when asking for things. But if you're ignored, don't be afraid to put a little bit of claw into your request.

88. Never try to push your head into any opening that your whiskers won't clear easily.

89. Inspire whimsy in
everyone you meet.

90. Chase and bite human toes through the bedcovers.

91. Ignore any endeavor whose primary goal is self-improvement.

92. Don't sweat the little stuff.

93. Don't sweat the big stuff.

94. Surprise the entire household by unrolling all the toilet paper at night.

95. Never yawn half-heartedly.

96. Never purr half-heartedly.

97. Never eat more than your own weight in table scraps.

98. Never let anyone dye your hair a funny color or give you a trendy haircut.

99. Eschew colored bows or plastic barrettes in your hair.

100. Spurn kitty clothes.

101. Ignore all fitness fads.

102. Say "Yes!" to armchairs, cut flowers, belly rubs, and tuna fish.

103. Remember—meow, and the world meows with you; hiss, and you hiss alone.

104. Force people to throw you off their laps at least three times before conceding that they actually mean it.

105. Don't play in plastic bags.

106. Take time to sit in the grass and watch the clouds roll by.

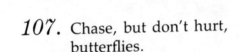

107. Chase, but don't hurt, butterflies.

108. No matter how old you are, never be afraid to express the kitten within you.

109. Keep in mind that just because a man or woman is poor or even homeless doesn't mean they can't be a loving and devoted companion. There is absolutely *no* correlation between money and a good heart.

110. Refuse to retrieve things.

111. Protest, in the strongest terms possible, any suggestion that what the household really needs right now is a new puppy.

112. Keep everybody's secrets.

113. Ignore your mistakes.

114. Scratch your ears regularly.

115. Pose for photos.

116. Bathe with a friend.

117. Learn to watch everything, even with your eyes closed.

118. Steer clear of wasps, bees, ants, and spiders. At best, they make iffy playmates; at worst, they're hazardous between-meal snacks.

119. Never join anything.

120. Persuade people to devote all their free time to petting you.

121. The three best rainy day activities are:

1. Sleeping
2. Napping
3. Taking it easy

122. The three best late-night activities are:

1. Chasing a pingpong ball around the bathtub

2. Dragging underwear, pantyhose, and socks from room to room

3. Climbing and hanging from the window screens while wailing loudly

123. Make friends with the milkman.

124. Be suspicious of anyone whose clothes are immaculate and completely free of cat hairs. It means they either don't like cats or don't hug the ones they have.

125. When in doubt, let your tail do all the talking for you.

126. Don't waste time watching television.

127. Don't waste time staring in mirrors.

128. Don't waste time trying to figure out the meaning of life.

129. Don't introduce yourself to new neighbors by sharpening your claws on their patio furniture or playing in their flowerbeds. First impressions can rarely be undone.

130. Drink lots of water.

131. Play and sleep in cardboard boxes.

132. Be inscrutable.

133. Be regal.

134. Be nobody's fool.

135. Resist an impulse to nap
in your food dish.

136. Help with making the bed.

137. Help with redecorating, even when no one asks you.

138. Help with making dinner.

139. For mild stomach upsets, eat plenty of grass. If that fails, try a little yogurt.

140. To stay warm on cold winter days, sleep on the sill of an east window in the morning and a west window in the afternoon. That way, you'll always catch the sunshine.

141. Refuse to tolerate being locked out of the bedroom for any reason whatsoever.

142. Shed your heart out.

143. Control your temper.

144. Avoid acting on jealous impulses, no matter how justified they seem at the time.

145. Try to avoid sitting around with your tongue sticking halfway out of your mouth; it tends to make you look slightly loopy.

146. Beware of water pistols.

147. Beware of lit cigarettes.

148. When kneading someone's belly, stop just short of drawing blood.

149. Push your luck.

150. Don't wait until Christmas morning to open the presents.

151. Don't whine when your toys disappear under the refrigerator or down the heating ducts. Accept the fact that life can be brutally unfair at times.

152. Never make abrupt moves. Always *insinuate* yourself into any situation, including a warm lap.

153. Don't just inhabit a house; become its *soul*.

154. Learn to develop a memorable meow.

155. Regard all neatly stacked piles of paper as an invitation to run amok.

156. Find any excuse to run up and down the stairs dementedly.

157. Retain your sense of wonder about all things.

158. Retain your curiosity.

159. Refrain from giving anyone a dead mouse or bird as a present; your idea of the perfect gift may not be somebody else's.

160. Don't throw yourself at house guests, no matter how receptive they seem; it compromises your dignity.

161. Steer clear of cactus gardens.

162. Learn to appreciate fine books—especially when someone else is reading them.

163. Never race across a recently mopped floor; you could slip and hurt yourself.

164. Don't cry over spilt milk—lap it up instead.

165. Become someone's friend
for life.

166. Bestow love bites sparingly and only to those who will appreciate the spirit in which they were meant.

167. Avoid chewing on pens or pencils: the ink and lead could poison you.

168. Always look astonished and perplexed when you break something, even if you meant to do it.

169. Always sleep under the covers. Humans will never throw you out if you snuggle under the covers with them.

170. Resist a temptation to claw strangers who make dense remarks like "Isn't it amazing? Every cat almost has its own distinct personality."

171. Don't waste time learning to do things that others will do for you.

172. Stay out of trash cans and dumpsters.

173. Lay claim to every jacket, sweater, and shirt as soon as it lands on a chair.

174. Always make sure the lid is down on the toilet before jumping on it.

175. Never swat the food right out of someone else's mouth—unless you're absolutely convinced they won't retaliate.

176. Tread silently.

177. Knock small things off of counters.

178. When a child starts screaming or crying loudly, resist a temptation to silence it immediately.

179. Never retract your claws completely, except with your very best friends.

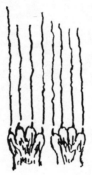

180. Avoid shoving your private parts in people's faces, no matter how much you think they like you.

181. Never bite the hand that feeds you—except as a last resort.

182. Never try to be something you're not.

183. Never give in to vulgarity.

184. Never be too smart for your own good.

185. Trust your intuition.

186. Become a paragon of sanity, sensuality, and contentment.

187. Sleep under table lamps.

188. Sleep on the answering machine.

189. Sleep in the middle of the hallway.

190. Learn to recognize the difference between the sounds of ordinary cans being opened and cat food cans being opened.

191. Always enter a room with poise and confidence. If you accidentally slip or stumble, stop immediately and start licking yourself rigorously—it distracts would-be hecklers.

192. Chase all shoelaces.

193. If someone breaks into the house when no one else is home, don't be a hero. Hide. Leave the heroics to dogs.

194. Remember: Everyone likes to wake up to a kiss.

195. Be bold.

196. Be winsome.

197. Be wildly tender.

198. Autumn leaves and news-papers were made to be played in.

199. Sleeping in the sunlight is often the best medicine for whatever ails you.

200. Make the world your scratching post.

201. Never sleep alone.

About the Author

LEIGH RUTLEDGE lives in Colorado, where he shares his home with 28 housecats, a number that will almost certainly increase with time. He has been known to save cats from storm sewers, unscrupulous pet stores, abusive owners, and busy interstate highways. He is also, incidentally, the author of *The Left-Hander's Guide to Life* and a humor book, *Excuses, Excuses* (both published by Plume). His manuscripts usually arrive at the publisher's office covered with cat hair.